MICHAEL REID

COLLEGE SUCCESS HABITS

The Ultimate Guide to Campus Living, Learn all the Information About Living On and Off Campus and How it Can Help You Have a Successful College Life

Descrierea CIP a Bibliotecii Naţionale a României
MICHAEL REID
  COLLEGE SUCCESS HABITS. The Ultimate Guide to
Campus Living, Learn all the Information About Living On
and Off Campus and How it Can Help You Have a Successful
College Life / Michael Reid – Bucharest: Editura My Ebook, 2021
  ISBN

MICHAEL REID

COLLEGE SUCCESS HABITS

The Ultimate Guide to Campus Living, Learn all the Information About Living On and Off Campus and How it Can Help You Have a Successful College Life

My Ebook Publishing House
Bucharest, 2021

TABLE OF CONTENTS

INTRODUCTION

College is a time for leaving the security and comfort of home. It embarks on the journey to adulthood. Unlike elementary or high school days, starting a college life is a little bit tough. By entering college, you will face new people and situations that would be extremely different from any you have previously met.

In college life, you also need to learn how to manage your finances, form new friends, learn new social skills and engage in a new form of thinking. Though college life is totally different from your previous school days, you will surely enjoy it. It is simply a matter on how you interact with others and how you adapt in your new environment.

Are you excited to enter in a college life? You should be! College life is probably the second best learning curve you have in your lifetime. A college campus usually consists of a major part of maturing and matured men and women, creating a perfect foil for you to educate various degrees of humanity life. It also gives you an extensive understanding of whatever you want to know.

For some, starting a college life can seem a bit strange. Others may also think that college life is a new face and adventure of their life. Whatever perceptions you have, you have to learn a few tips and tricks to ensure that you will survive and enjoy your college life. If you don't know how to make the best out of your college life, you are on the right spot.

This eBook explains how to enjoy and endure your college life. So, take time to read this eBook and see how it can help you!

CHAPTER 1

WHAT IS CAMPUS LIVING ALL ABOUT?

Synopsis

Getting ready for college can be nerve-racking. To reduce that nervous tension, get yourself as controlled as possible. You also need to make a checklist of what needs to be done before you leave in your house. It is also best to understand everything about campus living.

Living in a dorm is much simpler than living in an apartment. Like other students, you don't have to worry about monthly bills, no worries about groceries or cooking and a lot more. The main disadvantage is that your dorm can seem a bit overcrowded.

The Idea of Campus Living

As a college student, you should know what to choose from. What do you want - on-campus or off-campus living? Before choosing, try to examine these two types. If you have an insufficient idea about this topic, try to conduct your own research. As an option, you can also use the following paragraphs as your guide.

On-Campus vs Off-Campus Living

One of the critical decisions that students should take is to whether they will live at school or off campus. Students who desire to be close to the campus community choose on-campus living. But, students who want to be independent prefer to live in off-campus.

To give you some hints about the distinction of on and off campus living, here they are:

- **Social Opportunities** –Both on and off campus houses provide social opportunities. On-campus usually house hundreds of residents, including a major number on each floor. This offers an access to more people. It holds social events for residents to get together and the facilities usually features lobby areas or game rooms. However, apartment landlords expect that students will respect their properties. Thus, they need to follow their exact rules and regulations.

- **Living Space** – Living space in off-campus can greatly based on whether you live in an apartment or house. It also varies on how many roommates you have. The on-campus, on the other hand, is usually small. It has beds, desks and closets for each resident. This leaves little room for moving or lounging about. Thus, it offers little room for escape to solitude.

- **Costs** – Students shop around for off-campus housing to lower their cost of living. Whether you want to live in an on or off campus, the expenses might be the same. It only varies depending on the type of house you want to live in.

- **Campus Connection** – On-campus provides a much closer connection to the campus community. Thus, students who desire to get involved in intramural activities and club would benefit from this type of living. Off-campus students, on the other hand, restrict the convenience of getting involved in school activities.

After knowing what the difference of on and off campus living, you can weigh which of these two options suit your needs and budgets.

If you can't decide what to pick from, don't hesitate to ask help from your friends and families. They will surely provide the best advice to enjoy your college life.

CHAPTER 2

BENEFITS OF CAMPUS LIVING

Synopsis

There are various benefits to students living on campus. These countless advantages can be attached to access to programs in the campus and the relationships to the campus community provided by the halls.

Students who live in on-campus receive direct advantages related to individual academic success than to off-campus students. For your guide, here are the top five benefits of on-campus living you shouldn't miss to know:

In case you are attending college on a tight budget, you always want to have a part time job to sustain your regular expenses. Like other students, on- campus living can be your best option. Through this, it is easy for you to finish your job and attend at school on time. This can be done because your place is a few minutes away from your job and school.

Benefits

1. **Academic Impact** – Students living in on-campus experience a great impact to their lives. They are more likely to join in campus learning communities. As a result, they are more exposed to interact with faculty in residence through in hall study groups and special features. They also have a chance to enrich their experience beyond the classroom setups.

Experts claimed that students living in on-campus tend to earn excellent grades. They also have retention rates at their university. These students are also timelier in their graduation. They can also easily promote their growth by helping them to stay associated to the college environment.

2. **Time Management and Convenience** – Most students find that living on campus is more well-situated than off-campus. Unlike other students, they don't have to waste more time and money to arrive on time. Instead of spending for their transportation expenses, on- campus students can use their budgets to other personal needs.

For most students, on-campus living offers access to a wide variety of campus services. They also have a chance to interact more with student mentors and faculty members. Thus, they can take greater advantage of academic support services such as personal and academic counseling, advising, mentoring and a lot more.

3. **Personal and Social Development** – On-campus living integrates social and learning development. It provides students the opportunity to form a personality or a sense of neighborhood with the institution.

Students also participate in more campus activities, engage in leadership experiences and take the advantage of campus resources.

In addition, on-campus living also allows students to actively involve in campus wide organizations. They tend to have a wide personal understanding, witness positive changes and have higher self-esteem.

4. **Support for Campus Services and Events** – Students who opt to live in on-campus have a chance to get economies of scale for a variety of programs and services. Most students are allowed to have meal plans which offer a base for on campus food services three times a day.

Additionally, these students are more likely to reward themselves of campus support systems, campus recreational areas and campus facilities.

5. **Safety and Security** - Students inside the campus are totally secured. Most universities offering on-campus living have security guards. These guards constantly taking out the surroundings of the campus for suspicious intruders. These guards also monitor every student because allowing them to enter in the vicinity.

CHAPTER 3

WHY CAMPUS LIVING COST MORE?

Synopsis

Are you planning to budget your college expenses? Then, you need to decide on areas where you can save money. One of the main concerns of attending college is financing your living expenses. However, depending on the place that you live in, you may find a better deal on or off campus.

In some places, on-campuses may be a much expensive option compared to renting an apartment with your colleagues or by yourself. This only depends on where you live and how close you live to campus.

To give you some hints, simply consider the following:

Comparison Between Rent On and Off Campus

- **Costs of Extras** - In most cases, on-campus will cover all of your utility costs and internet fees. But, your monthly fees might be too high. As advised, you need to consider how much each of these expenditures will cost. In addition, you also need to decide if you will need to pay extra for transportation. This is often observed if you are going to live in off campus.

In case you have a car, you need to pay for gas, parking cost and insurance. You may also need to pay for taxi charges, unless you are planning to take a walk to reach the campus.

- **Daily Meal Plans** – You should not underestimate the cost of meal and food plans. These plans can be one of the most expensive aspects of campus housing. But, you may be able to save through choosing a plan with only two meals per day. You can also buy breakfast foods at a convenience store. If you live off campus, you can also bring your lunch to save money.

- **Other Factors** – Your lifestyle and the things that are the most essential to you will influence your decision. In case you pay every bill by yourself, you always need to pick the cheapest option. If you are a working student, your work may influence where you work and what is the best plan for your situation.

When it comes to actual costs, on campus is more expensive compared to off campus. But, if you know how to save money, you will never spend more cash every month. You also have a chance to save money while studying in a prestigious school.

Take note that living in on or off the campus is both expensive. It is simply a matter on how to control your expenses.

CHAPTER 4

MEETING GREAT PEOPLE LIVING ON CAMPUS

Synopsis

College is the best time for meeting new people. This is time where you build a strong relationship with them. College is also a perfect situation that groups similar ages with distinct personalities.

For students, whether seniors or freshmen, it is always a pleasure to meet great people and make new friends. However, not all college students know how to meet interesting and new people. To give you some hints, read the succeeding paragraphs as your guide.

Best Ways and Places to Meet Great People Living on Campus

1. **Residence Halls** - Living in on campus is somewhat similar to a summer cap. Assistants on every floor set-up, plan and conduct creative and interesting programs each year. These activities allow every student to meet new people. Each floor is equipped with a lounge, which can be a sweet meeting place to play board gamesor other bonding activities.

2. **Activity Fairs** – These are the best ways to participate in organizations on campus and meet great people with similar

interests. Most schools organize a sport fest and other activities to unite each student in the campus.

3. **Around the Campus** – There are various people everywhere and you can talk to them anytime you want. When students share multiple classes, it creates an easy conversation starter.

4. **Parties** - The environment in the party is upbeat, fun and energetic. Through this, you have a chance to meet people while having fun.

But, make sure that you are always cautious of your actions and don't easily trust anyone.

5. **On-campus Job** – Acquiring a job on campus is an excellent way to be in a position to meet colleagues and also get paid. Most universities are seeking for assistants at the dining centers and other related departments. Opportunities can even be found in the residence halls and becoming a community assistant can be an excellent job.

After knowing the possible places where to meet new people, you can easily say that you have a chance to meet valuable students in the campus.

How Off Campus Students Meet Great People?

Living off campus is quite hard, especially when you are looking for a new friend at college. However, by putting in a little effort, you will find it fun and thrilling.

For your guide, here are some simple ways to meet great people even if you are living off the campus:

- **Make a Conversation with a Classmate** – Most students keep on chatting with each other before having their classes. To make new friends, you can spend enough time to talk to them.

- **Join a Sports Team** – Sports are the best way to meet great people in the campus. There is companionship and usually allow you to chat with your teammates.

- **Join a Club or Activity Group** – Say for instance, if you really love reading, you can join to a book club. If you like dancing, you are free to participate in any dance program. This serves as your channel to find new people and make friends.

Aside from the above mentioned, you can also involved yourself in a cause that you feel fanatical about.

CHAPTER 5

DEALING WITH CHALLENGES
LIVING ON CAMPUS

Synopsis

Before planning where to live in, you have to consider various things. Whether you want to live in on or off campus, it is natural that you will be facing some challenges.

For on campus living, here are the common challenges that you might experience:

- **Costs** – Living in a campus requires enough cash. You have to monitor your daily expenses and you have to ensure that you have the ability to finance your needs. Depending on your preferred schools, you may as a discount fee or student incentive.

- **Privacy** – In some campuses, they allow students to have roommates. With various numbers of roommates, you will experience a privacy problem. Roommates share bathrooms, study lounges, kitchens and a lot more.

- **Limited Space** – If you have plenty of roommates, it is hard for you to entertain guests. This is often observed if your roommates have a visitor at the same day.

- **Safety** – Schools employ security guards to keep the place safe. But, unsafe behavior like involving alcohol still happens. Thus, you have to choose the best university that provides strict regulations for your safety and security.

Tips on How to Deal with Challenges Living on Campus

At first, you may say that living in a campus is a little bit challenging. But, if you know how to overcome every challenge, you will find it easy and fun.

Here are some tips you can do to deal with various challenges while living in the campus:

1. **Know Your Budget** – Before you decide living on campus, you have to examine your desired school. You have to

know if they are offering cheap and expensive fees. If you don't have enough money, don't pressure yourself. You can find some universities that offer cheap campus fees.

2. **Observe Campus Rules** – Every school has its respective rules, especially when it comes to on campus living. Thus, each student should follow these rules to avoid any problem.

3. **Create a Visiting Schedule** – If you have plenty of roommates, you can create a visiting schedule. Through this, each of you has a chance to entertain your own guests.

In some cases, the same issues can be experienced by students who are living off the campus. That is why, it is up to you on how to handle these challenges.

CHAPTER 6

WHAT IS SO FUN ABOUT OFF CAMPUS LIVING?

Synopsis

Living off campus can be an exciting and fun time. However, you should also be aware of your responsibilities and rights as a roommate, tenant, community member and neighbor.

As advised, always ensure that you are aware of your surroundings at all time. You also need to take all safety precautions to ensure that you have a healthy and safe living experience.

Great Things about Off Campus Living

There are several things you can experience if you choose off campus living and here they are:

- **Independence** – This is one of the greatest benefits of living off campus. Most students living off campus are not procrastinators. It means that they always ensure that they complete their tasks as soon as possible. They are also dedicated to load up their vehicles and drive to campus every day. They also have a great control over their schedule. Thus, these students have a better chance at balancing a part-time job while studying.

- **Save Money** – Since students learn to become independent, they will know how to save their money. As much as possible, they will never spend their cash to their vices. They also learn how to budget their available cash to meet their school and personal needs.

In addition, students living in an off campus are free to entertain visitors with no limitations. They can also invite their friends to study or do some other schools activities. However, they can do this with the approval of the owners of the apartment.

Factors to Consider when Considering Off Campus Living

If you want to experience off campus living, you have to consider various things and here they are:

1. **What Fire Protection is in Place?** - Studies have shown that there are various fire incidents on off campus living. Thus, you have to ensure that you pick the best place. You need to check the fire extinguisher pressure gauge. It is also best to examine the secondary exit if it is functioning or not.

2. **Check the Security** - Simply check if the place has secured lock doors and windows. You also need to conduct a research if there are previous incidents happened in the place. As advised, know if law officers are aware that there are college students live in the place and other related concerns.

3. **Analyze the Lease** – Make sure that you are aware with the lease. You have to know everything from the renting fees to the rules and regulations of the owner. You also need to know your obligation as a tenant.

After considering the different tips about off campus living, it is easy for you to decide what to choose from. Thus, you don't have to worry in case you want to live alone or along with your friends.

Living off campus gives you a chance to do anything you want. But, you have to ensure that you stay hard to get the best grades. Though you are living alone, you need to focus on your studies.

CHAPTER 7
WHY OFF CAMPUS LIVING
IS MUCH BETTER?

Synopsis

What to choose from? Is it on or off campus living? As a college student, you are probably thinking what to pick from. Instead of worrying about this concern, try to consider this chapter as your guide.

At the previous chapters, you already knew the different facts and benefits of on campus living. For unbiased info, here are the different advantages of off campus living:

Compared to on campus living, off campus allows you to do anything you want. You will not be held to the limitations and rules that those on campus need to follow. You also have various options to improve your surroundings. It means that you can use your desired interior decorator to make your space more stunning and effective.

Off Campus

In addition, if you want home cooking, you be able to plan and make your own dishes. You can do this without any restrictions. If you are living on campus, you have to visit the campus dining hall. Thus, you can save a lot of money if you are preparing your own meal.

Gives a Wide Variety of Accommodations

Depending on your choice, you can rent a studio apartment for yourself. You can also share a bigger apartment with others. Some college students even go together to rent a house. However, choosing the best place to rent depends on your budget and preferences for roommates.

If you choose to live off campus, you can also entertain your visitors with no limitations. Thus, you can schedule a daily visit from your friends, families or relatives.

Provides a Break from Campus

Some college students don't want to stay in their campus. This is the reason why they choose off campus living. Renting an off campus home provides a break from school every night.

Say for instance, if you prefer a quiet neighborhood than noisy dorms, then, off campus living is your best option. You can find a serenity and peace in your own apartment when your campus classes and other tasks are complete.

No Distractions

If you are living on campus, you will find it hard to study your lessons. Some of your roommates may be too noisy and you can't focus on the things you need to do.

In some cases, your roommates may also entertain their visitors while you are studying. This scenario is really annoying, especially when you have to finish your assignments as soon as possible.

Develops Sense of Responsibility

In the near future, you may pick your own house. Living in apartments near campus will allow you to establish a rental reputation. This also builds a credit history. As a result, you will increase your sense of responsibility. You will be the one to ensure that your rent is paid on time.

In addition, your living space and clothes are totally clean. You also don't need help from others to fix your mess. You are also responsible for preparing your own meal, buying your groceries, adjusting your own budget and a lot more.

Meet New People

If you are living in on campus, you can also meet a lot of people. But, it is totally different when you are living in off campus. In off campus living, you will meet people with different courses, ages, colleges, sports teams and societies.

CHAPTER 8

SECURITY ISSUES LIVING OFF CAMPUS

Synopsis

A college is supposed to be a nurturing and safe place. Thus, campus safety is a most important concern not only to students, but to administrators and parents as well.

Issues regarding campus safety are significant. In fact, Department of Education creates a site to compile and disperse information about campus statistic. For your guide, here are some security issues of students who are living in off campus:

Security

• **Malfunction Doors and Windows** – Some students living in off campus prefer to get cheap deals. They don't even bother if their preferred house is safe to live in or not. That is why, you have to check first of the windows and doors of the apartment. Know if they are fully fixed and not easily prone to any destructive element.

• **Poor Security** – This may be observed depending on the type of apartment you choose. There are some apartments with great security while others do not. So, make sure that you pick the best one.

- **Drinking**– Since off campus students are free to do anything they want, some of them have regular gigs at night clubs. They keep on drinking along with friends. As a result, they may prone from unexpected situation. They also failed to protect themselves, especially when they are too drunk. Studies have shown that there are various incidents involving drinking. Some student also died about of these scenarios.

- **Hazing** – This is another significant issue by most off campus students. With their great freedom, they prefer to join in various organizations. This includes fraternities and sports teams.

To prevent security issues, you have to be more careful in choosing the best place to live in. If you don't know what to choose from, you are free to ask help from experts. You can also ask advice from your relatives, friends and a lot more.

Tips for Effective Off Campus Living

Whether you are new to off campus living or not, you don't have to worry about. Simply consider the following tips for effective off campus living:

1. Pay your rent on or before its given schedule

2. Avoid damaging the premises

3. Notify the landlord when repairs are needed. You can print your request form and keep one copy for your records

4. Observe and follow city laws and local county

5. Inform your landlord one month before you move out

6. Don't hesitate to introduce yourself to neighbors

7. Don't make any extreme noise that can affect your neighbors

8. Take responsibility for your visitors and their behavior

Aside from the above mentioned, you have to respect neighborhood parking regulations and other related concerns.

CHAPTER 9

ARRANGING FOR YOUR TRANSPORTATION
TO COLLEGE

Synopsis

With market and price fluctuations, money is getting even tighter these days. That is why, it is essential to keep your finances under control. To ensure that you can save a lot of money while meeting your daily needs, you have to create a budget.

Organizing your budget takes a little time, self-control and patience. Whether you want to arrange your transportation to college or other related expenses, it is always best to consider the following tips:

Transportation

- **Make a Budget** – Simply ask yourself how much money you need to spend every day for your transportation. To do this, you need to record your monthly expenses. This can give you an idea of where your money is going. You also have to keep receipts from a soda at the gas station or other related receipts.

- **Know the Areas for Improvement and Start Budgeting** – Students spend money than they realize. If you know how to save your money, you will surely amaze how it changes your overall expenses. Say for instance, if you are living a few meters away from your campus, you can take a walk instead of riding in a taxi.

- **Know How to Cut Your Gas Expenses** – If you think that you are spending more money on gas, you have to cut it down. You can do this through choosing the quickest routes and performing multiple errands at a time. Then, expect that you will be surprised at the exact amount you can save.

- **Optimize Your Gas Mileage** – You can do this through running odd jobs in a single trip. Say for instance, if you have a SUV, try to trade it for a gas affable vehicle. You can also use a communal transportation. The typical examples of these are the subway or bus.

After considering the above tips, you are certain that you can save a lot of money. You can also organize your transportation expenses. As a result, you don't need to worry about your future finances. Using your savings, you can easily sustain your future needs.

CHAPTER 10

MORE FREEDOM WITH OFF CAMPUS LIVING

Like other college students, you shouldn't miss a chance to live in off campus. What makes off campus living as your best option? To give you some hints, here they are:

- **Short Commute** – If you are living near the campus, you don't have to wake up too early. Some students need to wake up early because they have to commute for several hours. They are also worried of traffic and other unwanted situations.

- **Campus Advantage** – Students who prefer to live in off campus can take the full advantage of campus activities. You can also do anything you want without worrying anything.

- **Be With Your Friends** –Off campus living allows you to hang out with your friends. Thus, you are free to entertain them anytime you want. Unlike on campus living, you have to follow the strict rules of the campus. You also need to weigh if your roommates have visitors on the same day.

- **Study with no Distractions** – When studying your lessons, make sure that you always focus on your notes. That is why, you have to choose off campus living. In your own room, you can study alone with no distractions.

Since there is more freedom with off living campus, you are probably tempted to find the best place to live in. Take note that whether you are planning to live in on or off campus, your main goal is to finish your study. Make sure that you will do everything to submit your projects on time and get excellent grades. Most of all, think several times before doing anything. Since you have all the freedom, you have to know what is best for you.

After reading this guide, you are certain that you can easily decide what you really want. You also have an idea on how to make the best out of your college life.

As you can see, college life is really amazing. This is time to make friends while building your own future. So, instead of worrying on how to enjoy your college life, make a right move now! Simply use this eBook as your guide and expect that everything goes according to your plan.

Printed by Libri Plureos GmbH in Hamburg, Germany